D1784055

The Planets

Lesley Sims

W

FRANKLIN WATTS

LONDON•SYDNEY

© 1993 Franklin Watts
This edition 2001

Franklin Watts
96 Leonard Street
London EC2A 4XD

Franklin Watts Australia
56 O'Riordan Street
Alexandria, Sydney
NSW 2015

ISBN 0 7496 4139 8

A CIP catalogue record for this book is
available from the British Library

10 9 8 7 6 5 4 3 2 1

Printed in Italy

Contents

What are planets?

Planets are huge, spinning balls of rock or gases and liquids in space. The Earth is a planet. The word planet means 'wanderer'. Planets seem to wander across the sky. They are orbiting the Sun. From the Earth, other planets look like stars. Unlike stars, they do not have their own light. They are lit up by the Sun.

▽ This is how the Earth looks from Space.

The Solar System

The Solar System is the Sun and the planets, moons, and other objects which **orbit** it. The Earth is one of nine known planets in our Solar System. It is the third planet from the Sun. The four planets closest to the Sun are Mercury, Venus, Earth and Mars. They are the **inner planets**. Jupiter, Saturn, Uranus, Neptune and Pluto are the five **outer planets**.

▷ The planets are different sizes. If the Earth was the size of a Brussels sprout, Mercury would be the size of a pea, and Jupiter would be as big as a pumpkin. The Sun is even larger than Jupiter.

▷ The planets which orbit the Sun. The inner planets have much smaller orbits than the outer planets.

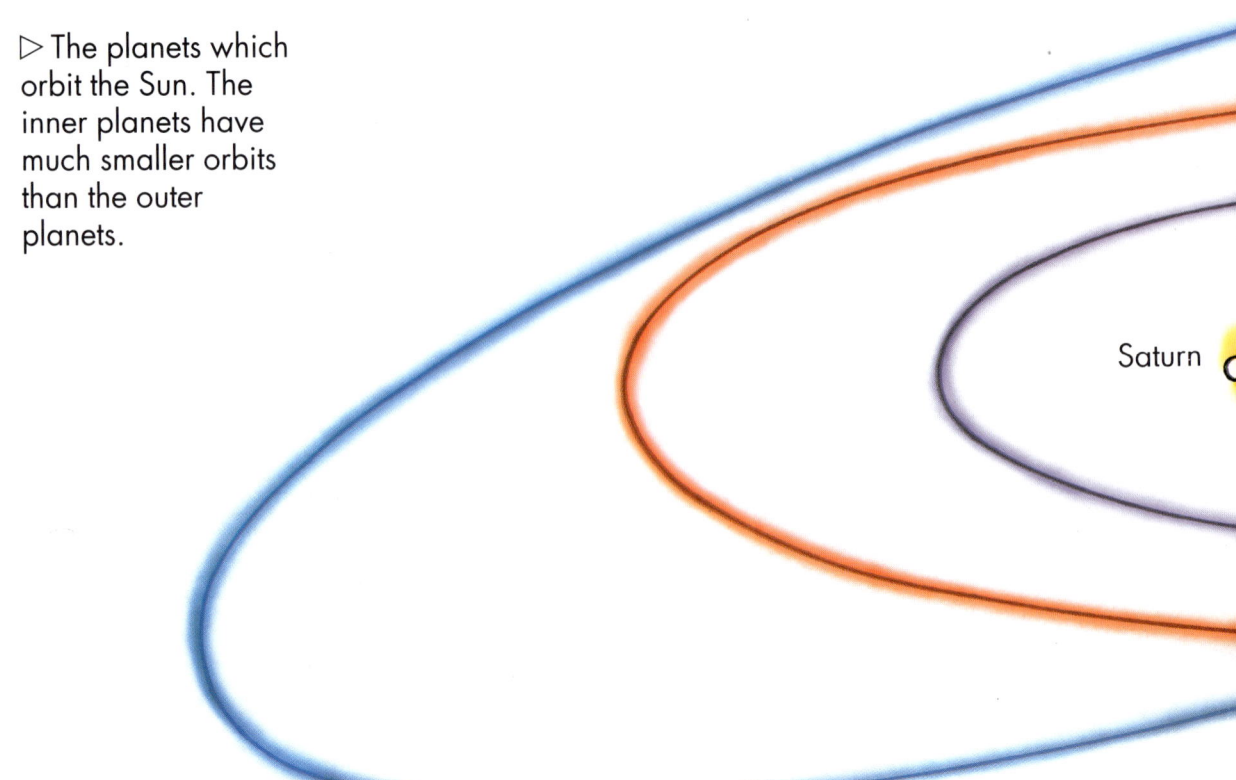

Saturn

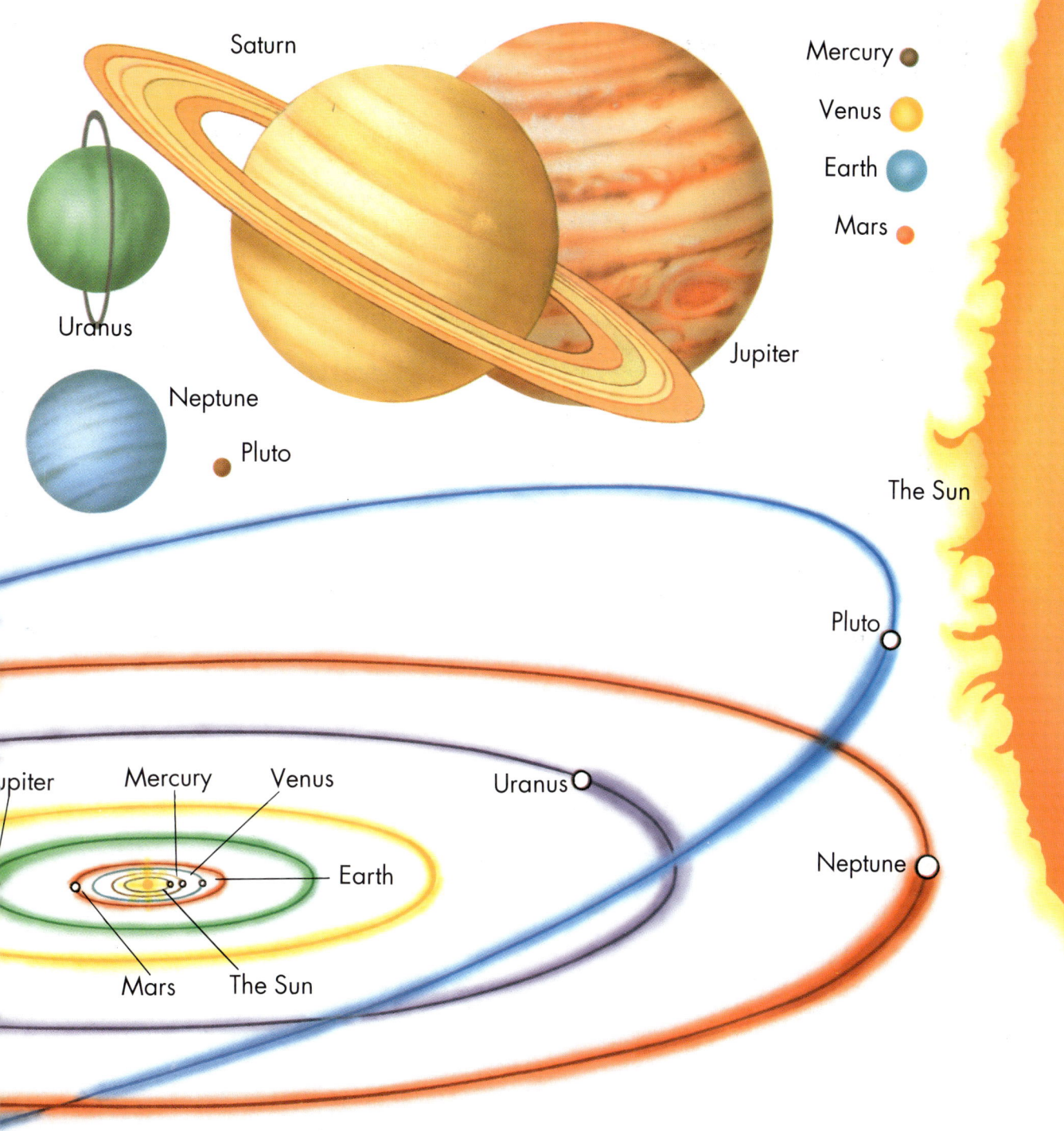

Saturn

Uranus

Neptune

Pluto

Jupiter

Mercury
Venus
Earth
Mars

The Sun

Pluto

Uranus

Neptune

Jupiter

Mercury   Venus

Earth

Mars   The Sun

5

Gravity

Planets are held in their orbits around the Sun because of **gravity**. Gravity is an invisible force which pulls objects together. Objects with a larger **mass** have a stronger force. The Sun's gravity pulls on the planets. The force of gravity keeps us on the Earth. Gravity holds **moons** in orbit around planets. Something in orbit is called a **satellite**.

▷ The Moon is a satellite of the Earth.

▽ People are lighter on the Moon than on the Earth. It has less gravity, because it has less mass.

△ The Moon held in
orbit around the
Earth.

The Big Bang

Most scientists believe that about 15,000 million years ago, everything was squashed together in one lump. Suddenly the lump exploded into millions of pieces. The explosion was so fierce, it threw the pieces far out into space. This was the beginning of the Universe. It is called the Big Bang. Millions of years later, one piece became our Solar System.

▽ Everything in the Universe, including this galaxy, formed as a result of the Big Bang.

▽ 1　A huge explosion.

△ 2　Lumpy clouds of gas and dust whirled through space.

▽ 4　One cloud became our Solar System. At its centre, a huge ball of gas formed into our Sun. The smaller lumps became planets.

▽ 3　As a cloud spun, it condensed and broke up into smaller lumps.

How the Earth was formed

The Earth began as a ball of hot, liquid rock and gases about 4,600 million years ago. Over millions of years it cooled down. The surface hardened into a solid crust. The gases cooled into rain which flooded the Earth and became oceans. The Earth's gravity held on to an invisible layer of gases which became air. This is the **atmosphere**.

▷ Oceans cover almost three-quarters of the Earth's surface.

▽ For its first few million years, the Earth was a very hot and violent place.

▷ The Earth is made
up of layers. On the
outside is the hard
crust. Underneath is
a layer called the
mantle. In the centre
is the core. Scientists
believe this is liquid
on the outside and
solid in the middle.

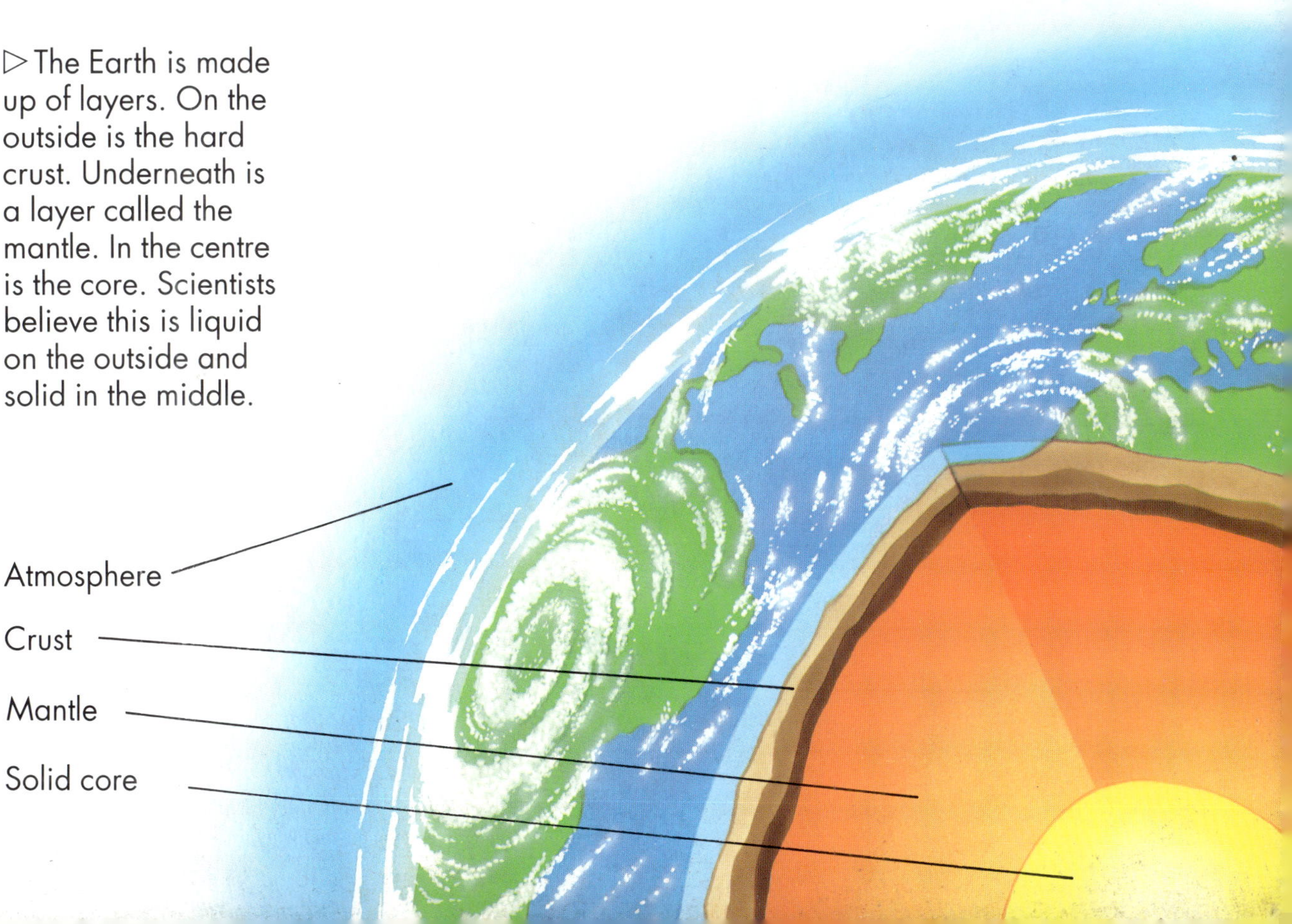

Atmosphere

Crust

Mantle

Solid core

Geology

Geology is the study of the Earth. The Earth's crust and upper mantle together form separate pieces called plates. If the rock at the edges of the plates moves, earthquakes occur. Volcanoes erupt when hot, liquid rock is forced through a weak part of the Earth's crust. Mountains form when the plates push against each other.

▷ A volcano can lie dormant for years, before suddenly erupting.

▽ An earthquake sends shudders through the ground, causing giant cracks in the Earth.

▽ Wind and rain wear away the Earth's surface. This is called erosion.

A year on the Earth

It takes the Earth a year to travel all the way around the Sun. The Earth tilts on its **axis**. At any one time, part of the Earth is tilted towards the Sun and is warmer. The part which is further away is cooler. As the Earth orbits the Sun, this cooler part becomes the part tilting towards the Sun and grows warm. These changes in temperature cause the seasons.

▷ The area around the Equator points to the Sun more than anywhere else on the Earth, so places on or near the Equator are always hot.

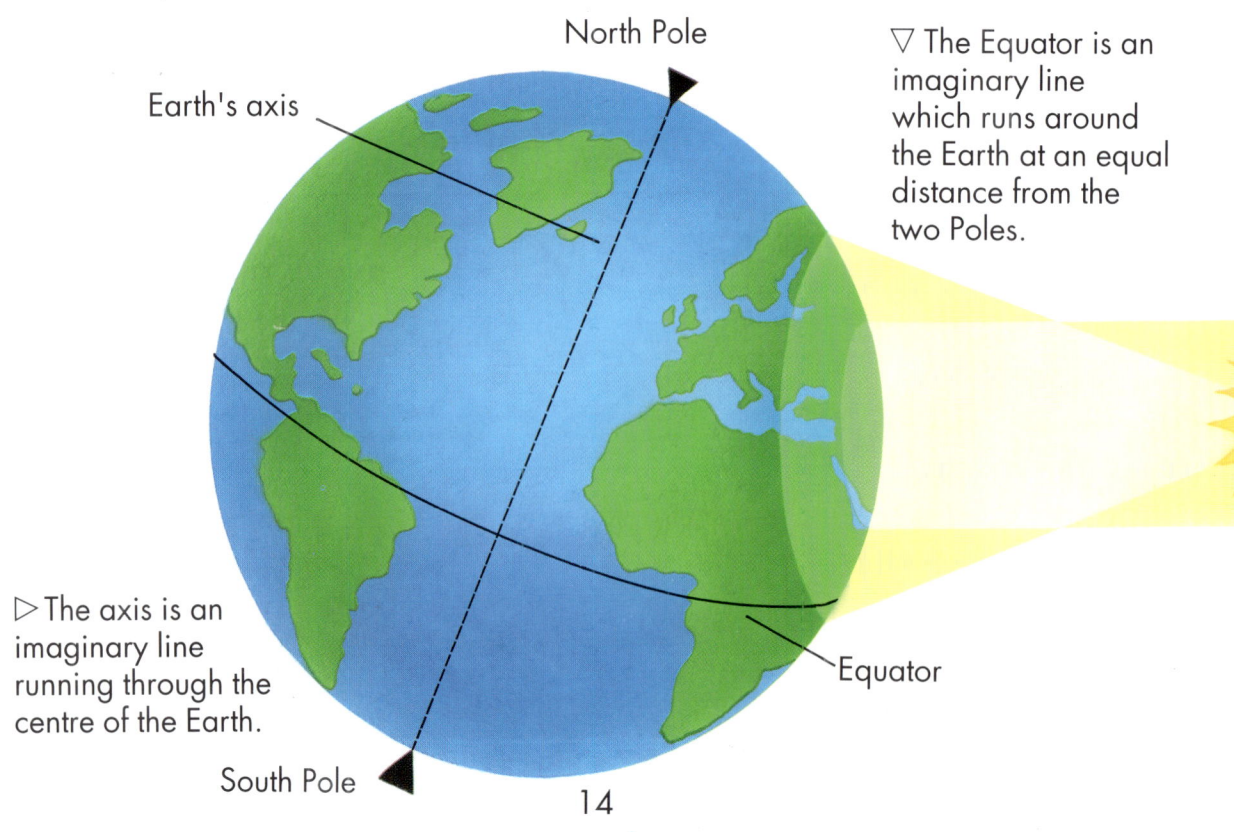

North Pole

Earth's axis

▽ The Equator is an imaginary line which runs around the Earth at an equal distance from the two Poles.

▷ The axis is an imaginary line running through the centre of the Earth.

Equator

South Pole

14

▷ When it is winter in the northern part of the world, it is summer in the southern part of the world.

North Pole ◄

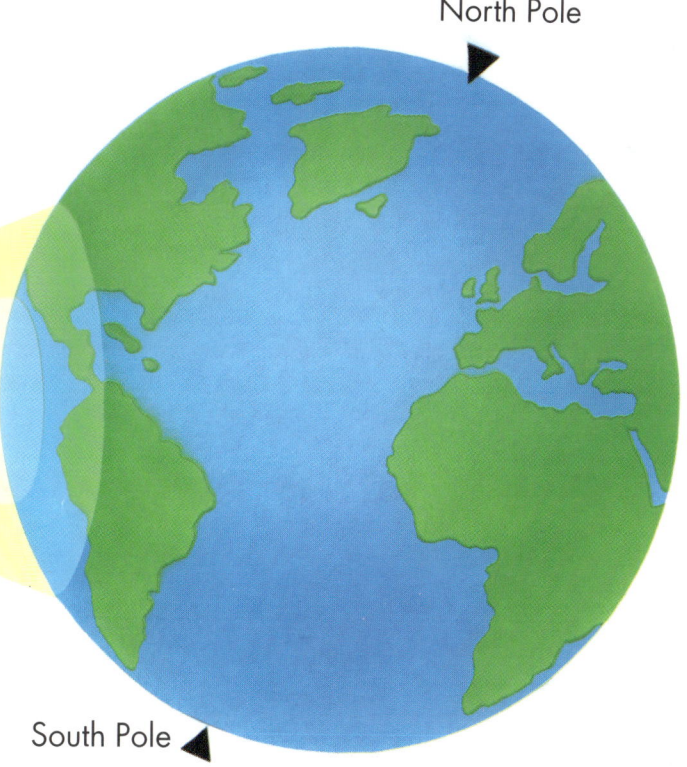

South Pole ◄

15

Mercury

Mercury is the nearest planet to the Sun. A year on Mercury is only 88 days long. Mercury is almost three times closer to the Sun than the Earth. On Mercury, it is much hotter and the Sun appears much larger than from the Earth. It is a dry planet, covered in holes or **craters**. Scientists think these were made by rocks crashing into Mercury when it formed.

▷ This spacecraft is Mariner 10. It sent back the first detailed photographs of Mercury to the Earth in 1974.

▽ The surface of Mercury taken by Mariner 10.

Venus

Venus is the planet closest to the Earth, and only a little smaller. The surface of the planet is covered in a thick layer of clouds, made of poisonous gases. These clouds reflect sunlight, so from the Earth Venus seems to shine more brightly than many stars. Beneath the clouds, Venus is rocky, dry and *very* hot. The surface is hot enough to cook on.

▽ America and the Soviet Union have sent robot spacecraft, called probes, to visit Venus. This photo of the surface of Venus was taken by a Soviet probe.

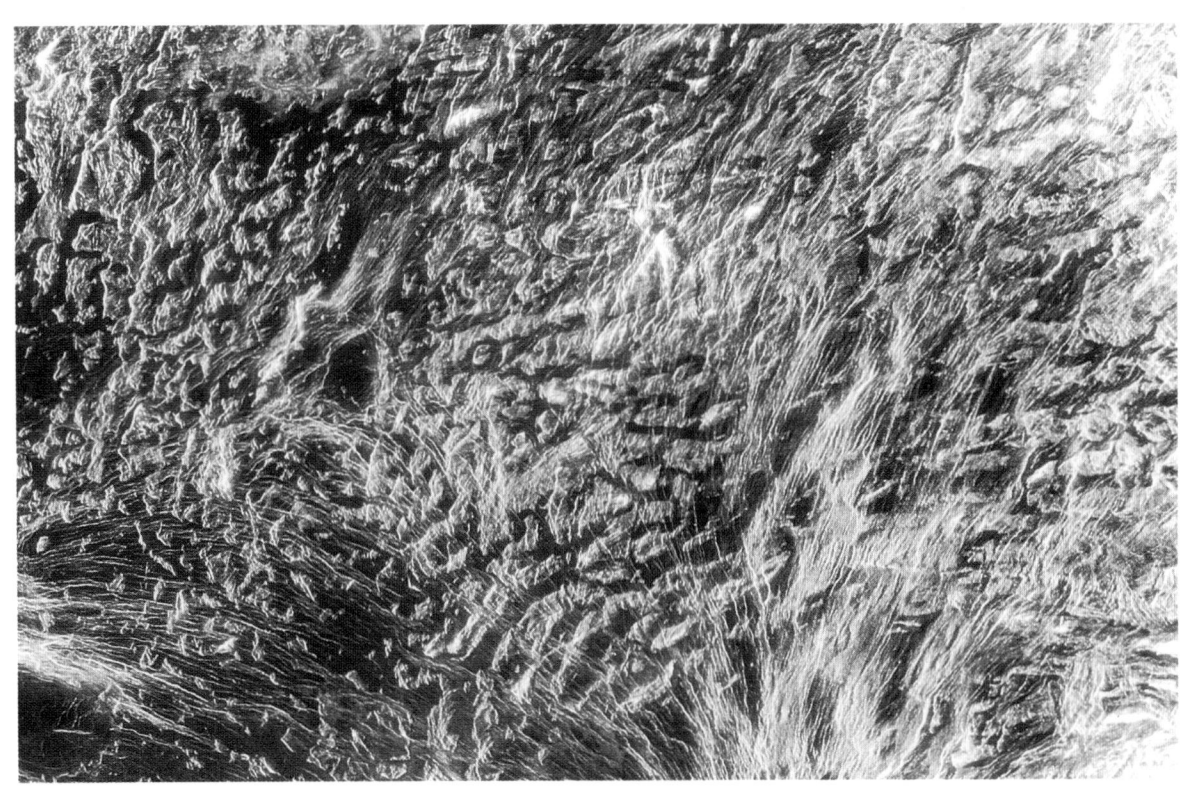

◁ Scientists believe the gas clouds surrounding Venus trap the heat from the Sun.

▷ This image shows what Venus is like underneath all the clouds.

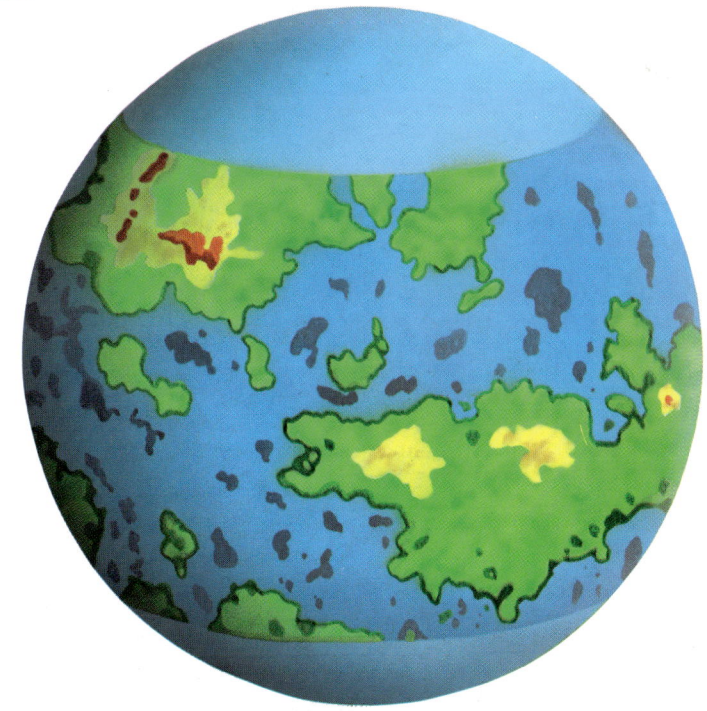

Mars

Mars is known as the Red Planet. Rusty iron dust in the rocks colours the surface a reddish-brown and turns the sky orange. Mars is a desert, but a very cold one. Dry channels run over the planet but Mars has no water on its surface. At the top and bottom of the planet are two white patches. Scientists think the water has frozen here.

▷ The surface of Mars, photographed by the American probe Viking 1, which landed on Mars in 1976.

▽ Mars has two moons, shaped like potatoes. They are so small they could both fit into one of the larger craters on our Moon.

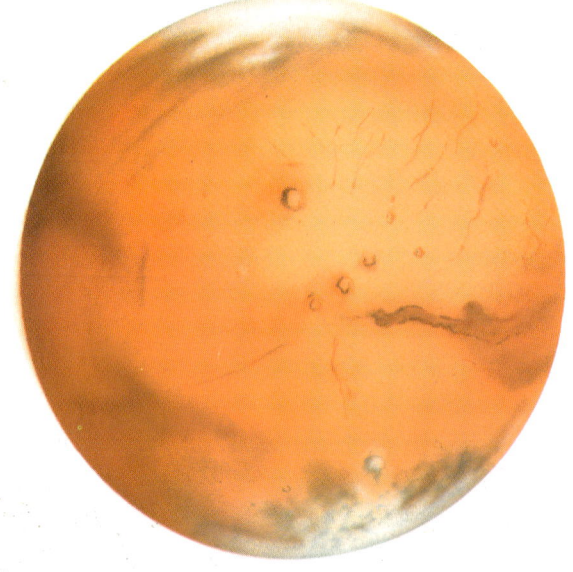

△ The ice patches at the poles of Mars may be more than a kilometre thick.

Jupiter, the gas giant

Jupiter is made up of gases and liquids, although it may have a small, solid core. Jupiter measures almost 143,000 kms across. It has more mass than all the other planets together. Jupiter has at least sixteen moons. One of them, Ganymede, is bigger than Mercury. Jupiter has a ring, but it is too dark to be seen from the Earth.

▷ The Great Red Spot is on the clouds which cover Jupiter. Scientists think it is caused by a storm, which has been raging for hundreds of years.

▷ This shows Jupiter with its four largest moons – Io, Europa, Ganymede and Callisto.

◁ Jupiter's moon Europa may be made of ice.

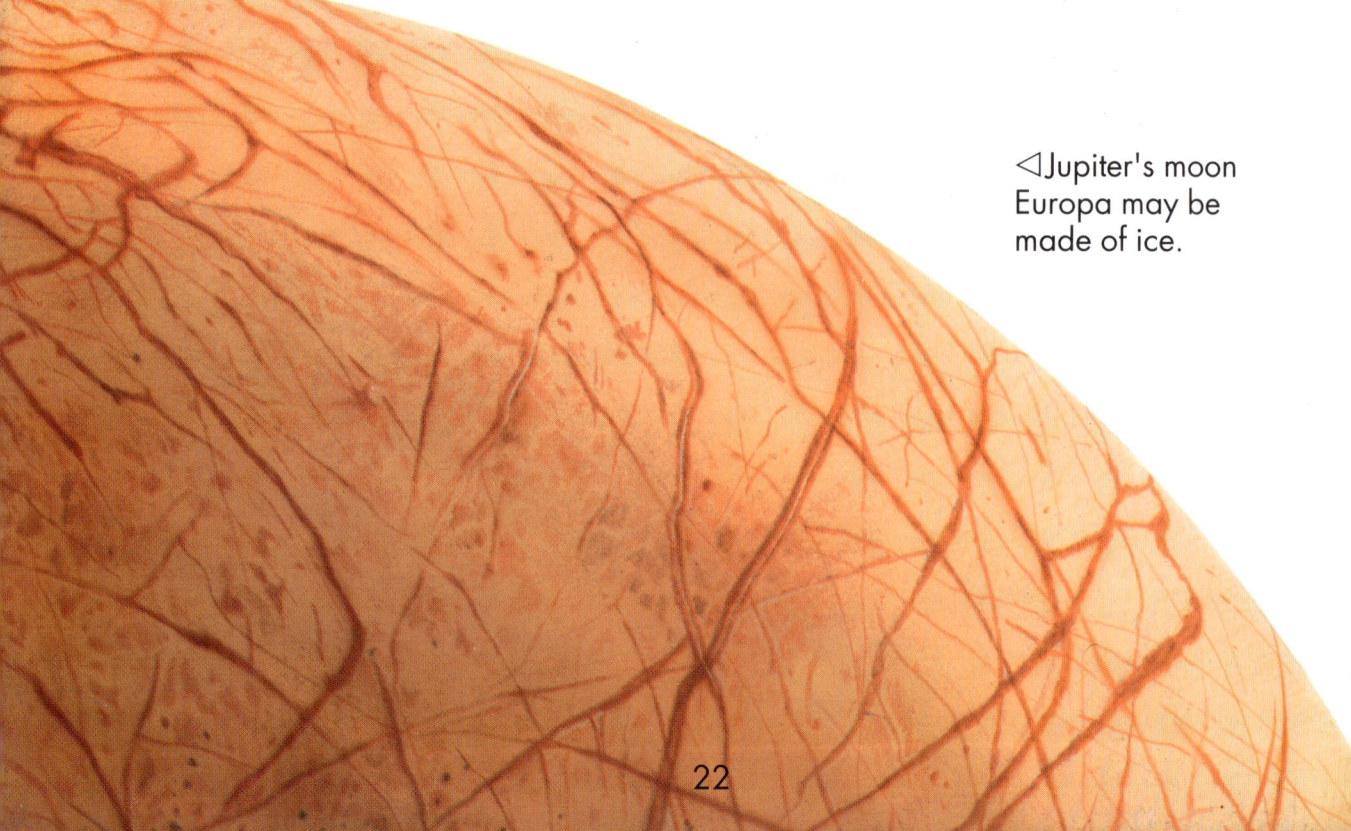

Saturn

Saturn is the second largest planet in the Solar System. It is another gas giant, with more than twenty moons. Saturn is surrounded by the most beautiful rings. They are made of tiny chunks of rock and ice which shine brilliantly in the sunlight. Even though Saturn is so big, it is very light. Saturn could float, if there was a swimming pool large enough!

▽ Although Saturn's rings are wide, they are very thin. Sometimes we can hardly see them from the Earth.

◁ Mimas is one of
Saturn's many
moons. It has a
crater which covers
almost a third of
Mimas's diameter. If
the rock which
caused it had been
any bigger, Mimas
would have been
smashed to pieces.

△ Saturn's rings
have lines that look
like the grooves in a
record.

Uranus, Neptune and Pluto

These planets were discovered with the help of telescopes. Uranus is hidden by a blue-green cloud of gas. It spins on its side. Uranus takes about 84 Earth years to orbit the Sun. A year on Neptune lasts over 164 Earth years. Because Neptune is so far from the Sun, it is very cold and dark. Pluto is smaller than our Moon. It has a tiny moon.

▷ Triton is a satellite of Neptune. It has volcanoes which spurt out gas. Frozen gas gives Triton a pink glow.

▽ Miranda is one of Uranus's fifteen satellites. It seems to be made up of lots of pieces, like a jigsaw. It may have broken up thousands of years ago and put itself back together in the wrong order.

▽ Uranus with its dark, thin rings.

Asteroids, Meteors, Comets

Asteroids are chunks of rock and metal. They are found in the Asteroid Belt, between the inner and outer planets. Other bits of rock and metal sometimes break through the Earth's atmosphere and burn up. They are meteors, or shooting stars. Bigger lumps which crash to Earth are meteorites. Comets are made of ice, frozen gases and dust.

▷ Asteroids are also called the minor planets. Ceres, one of the largest asteroids, is about half as big as Pluto.

▽ This crater in Arizona, America, was caused by a meteor.

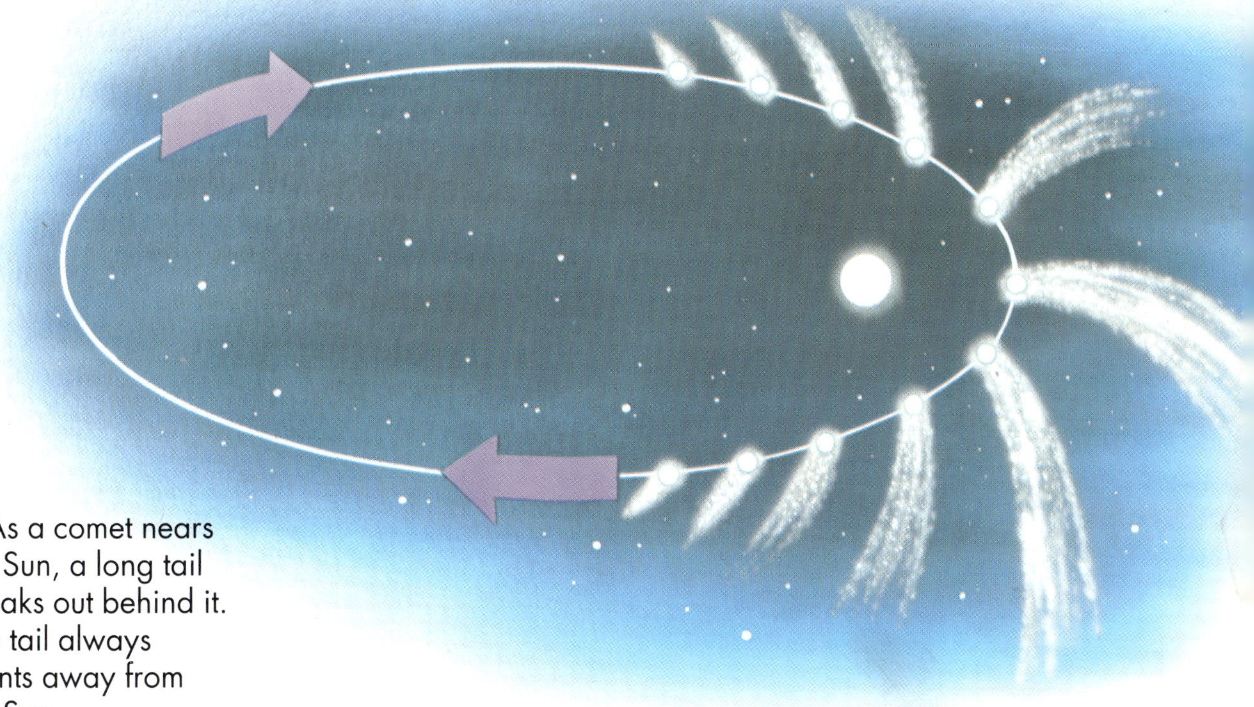

△ As a comet nears
the Sun, a long tail
streaks out behind it.
The tail always
points away from
the Sun.

Facts about the planets

- The Earth is the only planet in our Solar System that is known to support life.

- Scientists believe that in the next one hundred million years, the moon Triton will crash into Neptune and be destroyed.

- Pluto was discovered by scientific detective work. Astronomers could not explain the orbits of Uranus and Neptune. It seemed as though the gravity of another planet was pulling on them. The astronomers worked out where they thought the ninth planet should be. When they studied the sky, they found Pluto.

- There may be a tenth planet beyond Pluto, waiting to be discovered.

Glossary

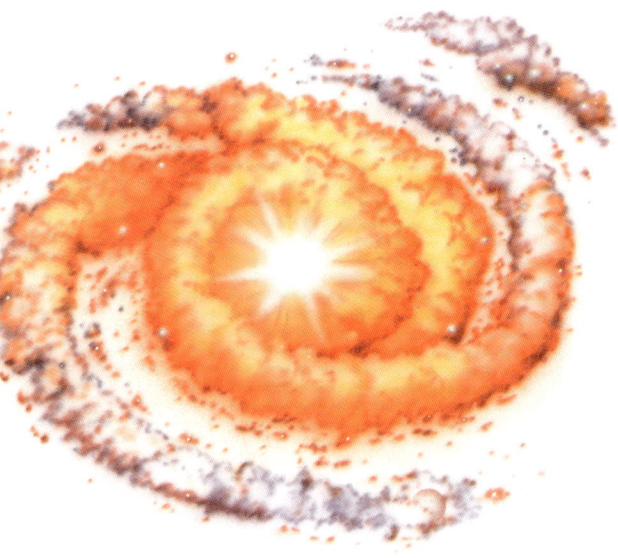

atmosphere The layer of gases which surrounds some planets. On Earth it allows us to breathe.

axis An imaginary line which runs through the centre of a planet, around which the planet spins.

crater A bowl-shaped hole.

gravity An invisible force pulling objects together.

inner planets The planets between the Sun and the Asteroid Belt – Mercury, Venus, Earth and Mars.

mass How much there is of something. An object's weight is affected by gravity; its mass is always the same.

moon A ball of rock or ice which orbits a planet.

orbit To travel around an object; the continuous journey of one object around another, such as the Moon around the Earth or the Earth around the Sun.

outer planets The planets beyond the Asteroid Belt – Jupiter, Saturn, Uranus, Neptune and Pluto.

satellite Something which orbits a planet.

Index

Photographic credits: Bruce Coleman Ltd 13; European Space Agency 3; Robert Harding Picture Library 7; Hutchison Library (Jeremy Horner) 15; Dennis Milon/ Space Photo Library 29; NASA 11, 16, 21, 23; NASA/Science Photo Library 18, 27; NOAO/Science Photo Library 8; TRH Pictures 24.